B.C.
Where the Hell Is Heck?

by
Johnny Hart

FAWCETT GOLD MEDAL • NEW YORK

B.C. WHERE THE HELL IS HECK?

A Fawcett Gold Medal Book published by special arrangement with Field Newspaper Syndicate.

ISBN 0-449-14022-9

Printed in the United States of America

10 9 8 7 6 5 4 3 2 1

1·18

JAKE, WHY DON'T YOU EXPLAIN SPORTS TO ME ...

.. THEN MAYBE NEXT YEAR I WON'T BE A SUNDAY AFTERNOON WIDOW.

OK! .... THE FIRST THING WE'LL TAKE UP IS THE TIGHT END.

1·30

WAS THAT THE FAT GUY AT THE END OF THE COUCH THAT THREW UP DURING THE SUPER BOWL ?....

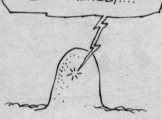

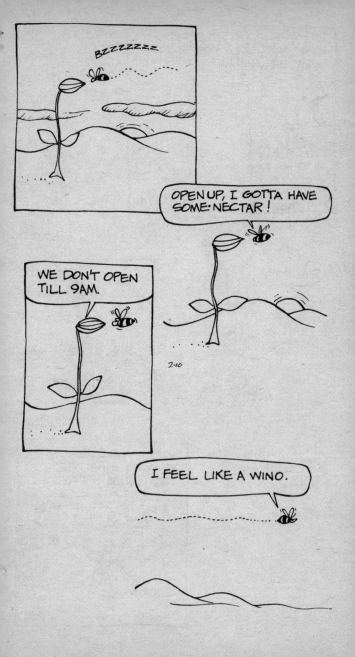

2·12

WHY AREN'T YOU IN SCHOOL?

WE GOT THE DAY OFF!

2·19

WHERE'D YOU GET THE CHERRY?

SOME DUDE IN A WHITE WIG CUT DOWN A CHERRY TREE AND GAVE US THE DAY OFF.

I DON'T UNDERSTAND KIDS TODAY,... YOU PUT ON A WIG, CUT DOWN A TREE, GIVE THEM THE DAY OFF... AND YOU'RE A "DUDE"!

2·20

2·21

WHAT GOES: WIFF-WIFF, LEAP
WIFF-WIFF, LEAP
WIFF-WIFF, LEAP

LET'S SEE...

OK,...WHAT?

A HURDLER IN CORDUROY SHORTS.

WHO GOES:
"WE'VE GOT TO STOP MEETING LIKE THIS!"

HMM.

3.7

I GNE UP, ...WHO?

ANYONE AND HENRY KISSINGER.

nait

WHAT GOES:
"PECK-EK-EK-EK-EK-EK
PECK-EK-EK-EK-EK-EK"

3.10

I GIVE UP.

A WOODPECKER ON
A RUBBER TREE.

3·14

3·15

Dear Fat Broad,
My neighbor, who works
nights, has a dog that
howls at the moon.

3.21

.... what can I do
about it?

— no sleep.

DEAR NO SLEEP,
BUY A DOG THAT HOWLS
AT THE SUN.

Dear Fat Broad,
Part of my neighbor's
Fig tree hangs over my fence
and ruins my grass...

ADVICE COLUMN

3·29

...what would happen if I
were to cut-off his limbs?
— aggressive.

DEAR AGGRESSIVE,
HE WOULD HAVE TO HIRE
SOMEONE TO PICK HIS FIGS.

ADVICE COLUMN

Dear Fat Broad,
My husband left me 3 yrs. ago, and I haven't seen hide nor hair of him since,

3.30

who do I contact?
— anxious.

DEAR ANXIOUS,
...EITHER DR. JEKYLL OR PETER RABBIT.

43

4-10

4-12

4.20

4-24

426

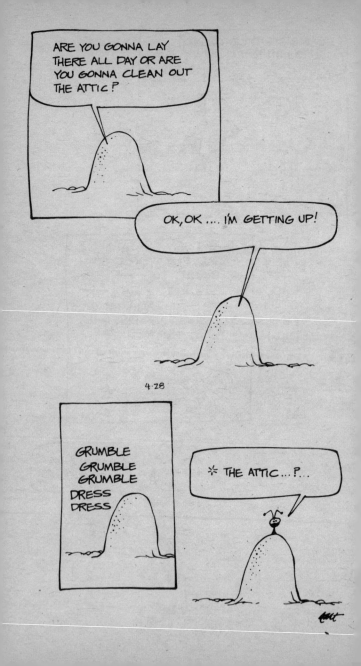

4·30

5·5

5.9

5-11

5·14

5·21

5·22

5·23

6·26

I'VE GOT A GREAT IDEA! .... LET'S FORM A WHEEL POOL.

WE NOT ONLY CONSERVE FUEL BUT WE SAVE MONEY ON TOLLS.

SOUNDS GOOD TO ME.

YOU MAY GO ON THROUGH.

TOLL 25¢

5-28

I'M SAVING A QUARTER, AND "THE AMAZING ZACCARINIS" ARE DRIVING A STUTZ BEAR-CAT.

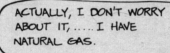

6.1

big·a·mist *n.*

an Italian's description of his last visit to London.

tee·to·tal·er *n.*

WILEY'S DICTIONARY

6-19

one who goes out on the golf
course as an assigned risk.

WILEY'S DICTIONARY

LOOK, LOOK, SEE DICK and JANE PLAN THEIR VACATION.

OH, LOOK, SEE THEM PLACE SPOT and PUFF IN THE KENNELS.

SEE THE KENNEL MASTER LAY HIS FEE ON DICK and JANE

6-25

SEE DICK and JANE SPEND THEIR VACATION VISITING SPOT and PUFF.

LOOK, LOOK, SEE DICK and JANE ROUGHING IT IN "YELLOWSTONE"

627

SEE DICK and JANE RUN OUT OF SUPPLIES.

SEE DICK and JANE IN THEIR BEAR SUITS BEGGING FOOD FROM the CARS.

SEE DICK and JANE GET LOST IN THE WOODS.

6·29

SEE DICK SAVE THE DAY BY REMEMBERING HIS COMPASS

SEE DICK and JANE SPEND THEIR LAST DAYS MAKING LITTLE CIRCLES IN THE DIRT.

SEE DICK RENT THE
SPEEDBOAT
SEE JANE RENT THE
WATERSKIS

SEE DICK and JANE
SPEED AWAY FROM
THE DOCK

6-30

SEE THE BOAT RUN
AGROUND

SEE THE DOC
EXTRACT JANE
FROM THE BACK
OF THE BOAT.

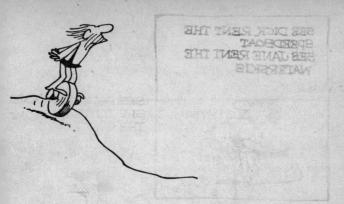

NO
SERVICES
THIS
ROUTE

7·3

EVEN THE CHURCH IS
SUFFERING CUTBACKS.

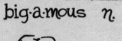

big·a·mous *n.*

7-4

an Italian's excuse for forcing a three-pound wedge of cheese into a mouse-trap.

7·5

7·6

1-7

LOOK, LOOK, SEE
DICK GO ON A SAFARI

SEE THE BEATERS AND
BEARERS CALL DICK
"BWANA."

7·10

SEE THE LION CHARGE
DICK.
SEE DICK APPEAL TO
THE BEATERS and BEARERS
FOR HELP

SEE DICK
DISCOVER WHAT
"BWANA" REALLY
MEANS.

SEE DICK AND JANE
SET SAIL FOR EUROPE

7-16

7·17

OH OH, ... THERE'S A VULTURE CIRCLING OVERHEAD.

MAYBE HE THINKS WE'RE DEAD...WIGGLE YOUR TOES.

7-21

NICE GOING ....HE JUST WINKED AT ME.

SEE DICK AND JANE SHED
THEIR WORLDLY BELONGINGS

SEE DICK AND JANE GO
BACK TO NATURE

SEE THE RANGER ARREST
DICK AND JANE FOR GOING
BACK TOO FAR.

SEE DICK FORGET TO
PUT THE CAMPFIRE OUT

724

SEE SMOKEY SNUFF OUT THE
FIRE WITH DICK'S FACE.

7.30

7-31

I THINK I'M IN LOVE ...

I'M SO MUCH IN LOVE, ... I CAN'T EVEN THINK STRAIGHT.

8-3

WHO IS IT?

WHO IS WHAT?

8-18

94

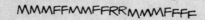

9.18

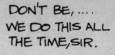

4.25

4·8

FAWCETT GOLD MEDAL BOOKS
in the B.C. series by Johnny Hart

$1.25 Wherever Paperbacks Are Sold